Liberty Phi

# SCORPIO

# INTRODUCTION

A strology is all about the planets in our skies and what energy and characteristics influence us. From ancient times, people have wanted to understand the rhythms of life and looked to the skies and their celestial bodies for inspiration, and the ancient constellations are there in the 12 zodiac signs we recognise from astrology. The Ancient Greeks devised narratives related to myths and legends about their celestial ancestors, to which they referred to make decisions and choices. Roman mythology did the same and over the years these ancient wisdoms became refined into today's modern astrology.

The configuration of the planets in the sky at the time and place of our birth is unique to each and every one of us, and what this means and how it plays out throughout our lives is both fascinating and informative. Just knowing which planet rules your sun sign is the beginning of an exploratory journey that can provide you with a useful tool for life.

Understanding the meaning, energetic nature and power of each planet, where this sits in your birth chart and what this might mean is all important information and linked to your date, place and time of birth, relevant *only* to you. Completely individual, the way in which you can work with the power of the planets comes from understanding their qualities and how this might influence the position in which they sit in your chart.

What knowledge of astrology can give you is the tools for working out how a planetary pattern might influence you, because of its relationship to your particular planetary configuration and circumstances. Each sun sign has a set of characteristics linked to its ruling planet – for example, Scorpio is ruled by Pluto – and, in turn, to each of the 12 Houses (see page 81) that form the structure of every individual's birth chart (see page 78). Once you know the meanings of these and how these relate to different areas of your life, you can begin to work out what might be relevant to you when, for example, you read in a magazine horoscope that there's a Full Moon in Capricorn or that Jupiter is transiting Mars.

Each of the 12 astrological or zodiac sun signs is ruled by a planet (see page 52) and looking at a planet's characteristics will give you an indication of the influences brought to bear on each sign. It's useful to have a general understanding of these influences, because your birth chart includes many of them, in different house or planetary configurations, which gives you information about how uniquely *you* you are. Also included in this book are the minor planets (see page 102), also relevant to the information your chart provides.

# SCORPIO

Our sun sign is determined by the date of our birth wherever we are born, and if you are a Scorpio you were born between October 23rd and November 21st. Bear in mind, however, that if you were born on one or other of those actual dates it's worth checking your *time* of birth, if you know it, against the year you were born and where. That's because no one is born 'on the cusp' (see page 78) and because there will be a moment on those days when Libra shifts to Scorpio, and Scorpio shifts to Sagittarius. It's well worth a check, especially if you've never felt quite convinced that the characteristics of your designated sun sign match your own.

The constellation of Scorpio is one of the largest in our skies and features the 16th brightest star in the sky, the red-coloured Alpha Scorpii. In Greek myth, the goddess Gaia sent a scorpion to attack the hunter Orion after he'd boasted that he could kill anything. Zeus placed the scorpion in the sky as a reminder that we should all avoid boasting about things we can't achieve.

Scorpio is ruled by planet Pluto, Greek god of the underworld, whose energy is all about the cycle of creation, destruction and regeneration, so although it's linked to death it's also linked to rebirth and what might need to die in order to be reborn.

A water sign (like Cancer and Pisces), Scorpio is fluid in attitude, but powerful with it when you remember how a drip of water can erode the hardest stone over time. It's also a fixed sign (like Taurus, Leo and Aquarius) that shows commitment and endurance, seeing things through to completion, and with the perseverance to stay on course. There is a powerful creative energy in Scorpio that also runs deep, and much appears to be hidden, secretive even, but that's because Scorpio prefers not to disclose any information until they are sure of it. There is also a deep need for calm and many Scorpios will occasionally withdraw socially to achieve this, which is often misunderstood and mistaken for moodiness.

The sign ♏ of Scorpio shows the sting in the tail, attached to a representation of the genitals. It is also the sign previously used for the mythical phoenix, a bird that could regenerate from the flames of its own destruction.

PHYSICAL POWER
Scorpio rules the genitals and the reproductive system and is associated with problems that can arise with fertility in both men and women.

SACRED GEMSTONE
For Scorpio this is the Topaz, and the yellow Topaz in particular, which is healing and strongly regenerative, helping Scorpio to focus light and energy when needed to restore their life force.

OPPOSITE SIGN
Taurus

Scorpio is depicted by the scorpion, a tough protective exoskeleton complete with a sting in its tail, and this is how many born under this sign are often seen, and see themselves. But this defensive armour is designed to protect an emotional side to Scorpio that can be easily hurt. These contradictions lie at the heart of Scorpio, who is often described paradoxically as powerful, weak, emotional, unemotional, clingy and independent, so it's not always easy to know which Scorpio will show up. And a fixed water sign can sometimes turn into a block of ice, freezing everyone out until they thaw again, giving them a reputation for being moody. But this is the constant cycle of change that many Scorpios have to live with, as do those they love.

Blame Pluto for Scorpio's hidden depths maybe, but they come with a deep spirituality and imagination, full of emotional empathy, and it's all too easy for Scorpio to become overwhelmed, hence the need for self-protection. As they mature, this all becomes much easier to manage but for some Scorpio children it can be a struggle to find their feet in a social group.

What is often underestimated is how affectionate and loving Scorpio can be, and how able they are to form good, restorative attachments. There's always room for change and regeneration here, and that too is within Pluto's gift, which every Scorpio must learn to recognise and trust in order not to constantly sting themselves. Idealism is another trait, and Scorpio can be idealistic to a fault, constantly seeking out all the possibilities of the good and the positive on which to build their foundation.

Loyalty too is a feature and as a friend, work colleague or lover, this is a real gift that can be taken for granted from most Scorpios. The other side of that loyalty and commitment is sometimes jealousy, and many Scorpios can be possessive about those that they love. It is part of their passion and intensity, along with terrific motivation and endurance, but this can also make Scorpio very competitive, not only with adversaries but also with friends, family, work colleagues and even lovers. When this passion is tempered by empathy and affection it can be very positive and Scorpio benefits, but it can have a darker side that can be self-destructive.

What's sometimes tricky for Scorpio to manage is the intensity with which they tend to approach every aspect of life. It can be very much all or nothing, black or white, up or down, with little middle ground. Luckily, as Scorpio matures, they become more philosophical and reinvent themselves time and time again, cutting themselves some slack and taking a gentler approach. Then these extremes can soften and they learn the subtle art of compromise, enjoying an easier life.

# THE MOON IN YOUR CHART

While your zodiac sign is your sun sign, making you a sun sign Scorpio, the Moon also plays a role in your birth chart and if you know the time and place of your birth, along with your birth date, you can get your birth chart done (see page 78). From this you can discover in which zodiac sign your Moon is positioned in your chart.

The Moon reflects the characteristics of who you are at the time of your birth, your innate personality, how you express yourself and how you are seen by others. This is in contrast to our sun sign which indicates the more dominant characteristics we reveal as we travel through life. The Moon also represents the feminine in our natal chart (the Sun the masculine) and the sign in which our Moon falls can indicate how we express the feminine side of our personality. Looking at the two signs together in our charts immediately creates a balance.

# MOON IN SCORPIO

The Moon spends roughly 2.5 days in each zodiac sign as it moves through all 12 signs during its monthly cycle. This means that the Moon is regularly in Scorpio, and it can be useful to know when this occurs and in particular when we have a New Moon or a Full Moon in Scorpio because these are especially good times for you to focus your energy and intentions.

A New Moon is always the start of a new cycle, an opportunity to set new intentions for the coming month, and when this is in your own sign, Scorpio, you can benefit from this additional energy and support. The Full Moon is an opportunity to reflect on the culmination of your earlier intentions.

# NEW MOON
## IN SCORPIO AFFIRMATION

'I welcome the regeneration that each New Moon heralds and believe that every day represents a new possibility for positive change.'

# FULL MOON
## IN SCORPIO AFFIRMATION

'At the climax of transformation, I can shed the old thoughts and ideas that have held me in check, freeing myself for the new.'

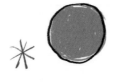

# SCORPIO
# HEALTH

Because Scorpio is aligned to creation and regeneration, this sign rules the genitals and reproductive system, not only sexual libido but also reproduction. This can sometimes link to problems with fertility in both men and women, but it also relates to the emotional side of creation which can be very intense with Scorpio. The link between emotions and the body can sometimes find Scorpio struggling to balance the two and becoming overwhelmed. So when it comes to Scorpio self-care, it's often a combination of both body and mind that can create problems and that needs solutions.

Given the way many Scorpios throw themselves into everything they do, whether work or play, there's often a risk of crashing and burning. Moderation isn't a word in Scorpio's vocabulary. They always assume that they are made of steel, physically and emotionally, and if they put their mind to it they can do anything. One simple way to help pace themselves is for Scorpio to literally walk and not run, and to ground themselves through regular, therapeutic walking. This is probably better than stylised meditative practices that can take them in too deep: with Scorpio it's always better to connect the body to the mind to help rebalance things.

# POWER UP YOUR SCORPIO ENERGY

There are often moments or periods when we feel uninspired, demotivated and low in energy. At these times it's worth working with your innate sun sign energy to power up again, and paying attention to what Scorpio relishes and needs can help support both physical and mental health.

Scorpio tends to get very caught up in their own thoughts and can sometimes become rather overwhelmed by their own ruminations, something that can affect their mood and sleep and contribute in turn to low energy, anxiety and depression. Physical activity can help break this cycle and lift mood, even if it's only the discipline of a short daily walk outside initially. Building on that by renewing interest in the external world also gives Scorpio a new focus and to make new connections, both with other people, ideas and places, and within themselves. All of which helps shift perspective, regenerating Scorpio's energy and engagement with the world.

Exercise always helps to reconnect body and mind, raising feel-good hormones and restoring fitness levels, contributing to the self-care that every Scorpio needs to prioritise from time to time.

Many Scorpios are familiar with their own cycles of mood and for some this can also include seasonal affective disorder (SAD) where they are affected by lack of exposure to light during the winter months. Having a plan to get through this cycle should include keeping regular hours to help support Scorpio's internal body clock and daily exposure to full-spectrum light from daylight (or a lamp). Physical exercise and regular nutritious meals also help keep Scorpio's circadian rhythm in sync, helping to avoid SAD too.

As a water sign, Scorpio can also try to support themselves with intoxicating substances like alcohol, or other mind-altering substances, but these can often aggravate rather than improve the cycle. Taking care to prioritise low-glycaemic carbohydrates in the diet – for example, oats, full grain cereals, bread and pastas, lentils and other pulses – helps stabilise blood-sugar levels, as does combining carbs with protein. Scorpio should avoid eating erratically to compensate for low energy and try snacking on fruit and nuts rather than junk food to keep blood-sugar levels steady. Keeping hydrated also helps Scorpio, but avoid highly caffeinated stimulants. Look to more subtle herbs and spices like cayenne pepper, chives and ginger to stimulate the palate, and coriander (cilantro), turmeric and parsley to detoxify the body.

Utilise a New Moon in Scorpio with a ritual to set your intentions and power up: light a candle, use essential oil of lavender to calm and boost mood (this oil blends well with soothing jasmine and uplifting neroli), focus your thoughts on the change you wish to see and allow time to meditate on this. Place your gemstone (see page 13) in the moonlight. Write down your intentions and keep in a safe place. Meditate on the New Moon in Scorpio affirmation (see page 21).

At a Full Moon in Scorpio you will have the benefit of the Sun's reflected light to help illuminate what is working for you and what you can let go, because the Full Moon brings clarity. Focus on this with another ritual, taking the time to meditate on the Full Moon in Scorpio affirmation (see page 21). Light a candle, place your gemstone in the moonlight and make a note of your thoughts and feelings, strengthened by the Moon in your sign.

# SCORPIO'S
# SPIRITUAL
# HOME

K nowing where to go to replenish your soul and recharge
your batteries both physically and spiritually is important
and worth serious consideration. For some Scorpios, their
spiritual home will always be linked to somewhere in the world
that's recognised as a spiritual place, where the earth's energy
resonates with their own, or somewhere they've created or recreated
explicitly for themselves.

Wherever they hail from or end up, there are also a number of
countries where Scorpio will feel comfortable, whether they choose
to go there to live, work or just take a holiday. These countries
include Egypt with its secrets of the mummies, beautiful, watery
Norway or mystical Peru.

When it comes to holidays, underwater exploration, regenerative
wellbeing holidays or snowboarding can appeal. You might find
Scorpio deep-sea diving in the Seychelles or trekking in Machu
Picchu, which are both locations that resonate with Pluto energy.
It can also be useful for Scorpio to balance the deeper side of their
psyche with lighter occupations, for example on cultural retreats in
Italy or Greece.

# SCORPIO

## WOMAN

This is a woman who catches the eye, often combining an intense stillness with a penetrating gaze. Scorpio women tend to move fast or remain stock still, almost as if they were waiting to strike. And generally, when they do move, it's brisk and purposeful. They may also choose orange or flame-coloured clothes or accessories, almost as a warning sign, while other Scorpio women are more subdued, avoiding attention and keeping their power secreted and under wraps. What is true is that most Scorpio women like to operate very much on their own terms.

Part of Scorpio woman's unique allure is their air of mystery. She seldom broadcasts her intentions, preferring instead to present herself when she's completely ready. Some might call her a smooth operator, but this belies how much time and trouble she will take, often in secret, before she makes her move because most Scorpio women know the value of preparation and, to some extent, performance. They are often very polished both socially and in the workplace, with impeccable standards.

All of which can create an air of 'look, but don't touch' which can sometimes obscure how affectionate, fun and loyal Scorpio women can also be, to their family, friends, work colleagues and lovers. But, and this is important, her memory runs as deep as her emotions and it's often hard for Scorpio women to forget past hurts. It can take some of them several cycles to regenerate their self-confidence once it's been knocked, and she knows this can make her vulnerable. Consequently, Scorpio women can be rather guarded emotionally, with something of a quick verbal retort if someone gets too close or offends her.

Like the other water signs, Scorpio women can be very sensitive to the emotions of others. For some, this can become overwhelming, and a balance needs to be struck. As they mature, many Scorpio women learn to set the boundaries necessary to prevent problems, without losing their empathy and compassion. As a fixed sign, it's not always easy to get this balance right, but it's important to avoid being overwhelmed by others' problems or demands.

S C O R

R

N

M A

P I O

Usually attractive to everyone, including children and sometimes even animals, there's something really rather magnetic about most Scorpio men. It's partly their stillness, which can make them appear very unthreatening in spite of that possible sting in their tail, and they tend to focus exclusively on a person, making them feel special. This intensity of attention can sometimes be misinterpreted as seductive, but that's just how Scorpio tends to communicate, sometimes masking the deeper emotional response that can be a feature of this sign.

This is possibly why Scorpio men have been considered among the Casanovas of the zodiac, which is a little unfair because they can be the most loyal and committed of men. But because their emotions run deep, they can instinctively move to protect themselves by often being less than open about their own feelings or intentions.

What many Scorpio men do occasionally need, however, is emotional time out. This emotional opting out can be a protective measure, and it's not easy for others to always accept it. What's useful is for Scorpio men to communicate how they are feeling, and finding the words to share their emotions rather than shutting down will usually be very helpful to them and avoid alienating others. As they mature, this comes more easily to Scorpio men, many of whom have the benefit of intuition to work with too. Learning to trust their emotions rather than hide from them can come from being more open to how they feel, and sharing those feelings.

Accepting that their emotions are also a source of strength, and understanding the deep source of this strength they provide, will enable many Scorpio men to flourish. There's a powerful energy to be utilised and this is often seen in the roles undertaken as Scorpio men mature, supporting others with empathy and compassion without feeling undermined. Then they can also regenerate their lighter-hearted, fun side with confidence, enjoying the balance and fulfilment this will bring to their lives.

# SCORPIO
# IN LOVE

Considered one of the most seductive of the sun signs, Scorpio can also give the impression of being unattainable, even while exercising their magnetic charm, and it can sometimes be a little mysterious to those on the receiving end. This paradox is partly because Scorpio tends to protect themselves emotionally, and can be quite reserved at first until they are ready to make their move. This initial reserve hides a passionate nature capable of turning love into an art form, and many Scorpios are not above playing games in pursuit of those whom they love. Intuition plays a part too, with many Scorpios relying on their gut instinct about whether or not a prospective lover is right for them. And being a fixed sign can make Scorpio peculiarly tenacious in pursuit, but it's done with such charm and persuasive tactics it's difficult to resist.

# SCORPIO
# AS A LOVER

Ruling the genitals and consequently the libido gives Scorpio the reputation of being a great lover or of being sexually promiscuous, but because of their deeper, emotional side, love can sometimes border on the sacred. For many Scorpios there's also a spiritual connection with the life force that sex can represent, the physical union that could create new life. For some Scorpios, there's often an unconscious connection with this, so they are not a sign that tends to be dismissive about the power of physical love. They respect its bonding and regenerative nature and the way in which together with their partner they can find and re-find themselves.

Fortunately, there's often an earthy counterpart to Scorpio's spiritual nature (remember, their opposite sign is Taurus) and Scorpio lovers can also see the fun and funny side of sex, enjoying it for pure pleasure rather than as a constant rehearsal for creating new life. Scorpio is often uncomplicated in the bedroom; they know what they like and part of that is that their partner enjoys it too, and they seldom make a secret of this. There's often a sensuality too, that goes beyond sex, and Scorpio is often able to show their love independently of sex, in deeds as well as in bed.

What Scorpio sometimes needs is sexual reassurance, especially if they feel threatened, and that's when they might react with a bit of a sting in the tail. Jealousy can sometimes cause problems too, and this can stem from the same need for reassurance. With maturity and life experience, many Scorpio lovers relax and they are also likely to remain sexually active with their partners throughout life, constantly regenerating and reinvigorating their sex lives.

WHAT'S IN SCORPIO'S BEDSIDE CABINET?
Stimulating water-based lubricant
A collection of erotic love poetry
Rampant rabbit vibrator

# WHICH SIGN
# SUITS SCORPIO?

In relationships with Scorpio, the sun sign of the other person and the ruling planet of that sign can bring out the best, or sometimes the worst, in a lover. Knowing what might spark, smoulder or suffocate love is worth closer investigation, but always remember that sun sign astrology is only a starting point for any relationship.

# SCORPIO
## AND ARIES

Mars and Pluto can be quite
confrontational together and Aries
can sometimes get a little exasperated
by Scorpio's deep thinking and
possessiveness, but if the water sign
can temper the fire a little, their
physical energies can supercharge
this relationship.

# SCORPIO
## AND TAURUS

Opposites often attract, and Venus
can be easily mesmerised by Pluto's
mysterious ways, and as long as
they don't both get too fixed or
confrontational in their own ideas,
Taurus can provide a very secure
base for Scorpio.

# SCORPIO
## AND GEMINI

Flighty Mercury can sometimes find
Pluto's depth-charged emotions
difficult to negotiate, but recognises
the value of the water sign's loyalty and
commitment, to which they find
it easy to respond and on which a close
relationship can be built.

## SCORPIO AND CANCER

The Moon reflects Pluto's gentler side, allowing Scorpio the chance to reveal their emotional vulnerabilities that Cancer respects and, in return, receives the security they often need in order to flourish in a partnership.

## SCORPIO AND LEO

The Sun's powerful ego can sometimes blind Pluto to the finer qualities of Leo, the fierce pride they take in those they love, but Scorpio recognises their desire to create a legacy, and together they can create an enormously strong bond.

## SCORPIO AND VIRGO

Ruled by Mercury, Virgo is an earth sign that has a practical approach to Pluto's mysterious side: they tend to ignore it and allow Scorpio the space to come and go emotionally. As long as they remain loyal, this can be a good match.

## SCORPIO
## AND LIBRA

Venus can have its work cut out trying
to balance Scorpio's emotional ups
and downs, and Pluto's darker side
might overwhelm, making this pairing
a tricky one unless together they can
find the space which both need.

## SCORPIO
## AND SCORPIO

They understand each other and can
probably manage each other's ups and
downs, as long as they avoid the potential
for mutual destruction, and they also
have the ability to constantly regenerate
the relationship they wish to have.

## SCORPIO AND
## SAGITTARIUS

Jupiter's energy can do a lot to lift Pluto's
deeper desires, as long as they can agree
philosophically, otherwise Sagittarius
may constantly leave and return. Scorpio
should be able to tolerate this, however,
given their understanding of the cyclical
nature of life.

## SCORPIO AND CAPRICORN

Saturn can be rather a taskmaster, but the goat's ability to continue on their path alongside Pluto's emotional upheavals creates the sense of security that Scorpio needs, while Capricorn gains from their more mystical, regenerative input.

## SCORPIO AND AQUARIUS

Pluto has huge respect for Uranus' unpredictability, understanding how instrumental change is for progress, although Aquarius' airy humanitarianism can make Scorpio insecure about their commitment to the relationship and may need reassurance.

## SCORPIO AND SCORPIO

Pluto and Neptune share a love of the deep, imaginative world of ideas. Their creativity is well matched, although there's a need to avoid overwhelming each other emotionally, but Scorpio' adaptability can be the key to success here.

# SCORPIO AT
# WORK

Scorpio is generally good at any work that's detail-oriented, because they like to dig deep and get to the crux of the matter. Whether this leads to a career as a horticulturist, market analyst or a 17th-century archivist will depend on their personal interests, but a superficial approach seldom satisfies this water sign. When it comes to teamwork, however, Scorpio prefers to be left to get on with whatever their task is, alone and uninterrupted until ready to share, and they need to feel trusted in order to deliver their best. In this way, they are reliable but Scorpio isn't always great at communicating everything their line manager may need to know, so it can sometimes require a bit of give and take on both sides.

Healing occupations can also appeal to this sign of regeneration, and this can be a hands-on approach for Scorpio, through nursing or medicine, or something more spiritual like reiki, or philosophical like psychoanalytic therapy. The mind, body and soul tend to be interconnected for Scorpio, and they find this concept an easy one when it comes to working with humanity, and the unconscious is familiar territory to them. Their empathy is quite pragmatic too, they don't particularly sentimentalise life and death, and many make good undertakers or clerics. That said, Scorpio is also as happy as a midwife, seeing new life into the world too.

Work colleagues generally find Scorpio to be loyal and hardworking, but problems can occasionally arise if there's a need to take emotional time-out, as this might not be obvious but can be misinterpreted as being shut out. But as they mature, many Scorpios find their lighter side and learn to manage that tendency to make a stinging remark (it may be justified, but some things are just best left unsaid), and not impose on others their deeper, more intense side. It can also take some time for Scorpio to find work that's really attune to their true self, and they may spend some time in further education or training, moving from job to job, until they find the right occupation for them to really flourish and be happy. Rethinking what they want to do, reinventing themselves time and time again, is all part of Scorpio's psyche and they generally get there in the end, although it's not always entirely clear to anyone else the progress that is being made along the way.

# SCORPIO
# AT HOME

Living with Scorpio can sometimes be like living with two people. When they are caught up in their own inner world, Scorpio can appear inaccessible, and at other times they are fully engaged. To an outsider, there may not appear to be any good reason for one or the other state of mind. It's not that they mean to disappear, but Scorpio's internal world sometimes needs attention. They may be tussling with a problem or sketching out a new project, but for some Scorpios it's an intense process and they can be completely unaware of how they are perceived.

Many Scorpios have something of a hideaway in their home, a place to which they can retreat to restore their energy. Their bedroom, or a study, den or even the bathroom can become a place of sanctuary. It may be softly lit, with comfortable furniture, womblike and relaxing. Scorpio's home may also reflect something of their sensual or spiritual side too, with soft furnishings and deep, glowing colours, silk drapes and woven wall hangings, plus spiritual artefacts from ancient religions or paintings with mysterious images and themes.

Many Scorpios also find the kitchen a place of transformation, somewhere to take simple ingredients and create a delicious meal. This is where a reclusive Scorpio can come into their own, socialising with friends over a meal they've prepared, having interesting and intense conversations. Spending time together feeding the mind as well as the body can be a real passion for many Scorpios, who acquire a reputation as an accomplished host as a consequence. This also provides an opportunity for Scorpio to show off their home and their domestic accomplishments, and for many it's here that they really flourish.

# FREE THE
# SPIRIT

Understanding your own sun sign astrology is only part of the picture. It provides you with a template to examine and reflect on your own life's journey but also the context for this through your relationships with others, intimate or otherwise, and within the culture and environment in which you live.

Throughout time, the Sun and planets of our universe have kept to their paths and astrologers have used this ancient wisdom to understand the pattern of the universe. In this way, astrology is a tool to utilise these wisdoms, a way of helping make sense of the energies we experience as the planets shift in our skies.

'A physician without a knowledge of astrology has no right to call himself a physician,' said Hippocrates, the Greek physician born in 460 BC, who understood better than anyone how these psychic energies worked. As did Carl Jung, the 20th-century philosopher and psychoanalyst, because he said, 'Astrology represents the summation of all the psychological knowledge of antiquity.'

THE 10 PLANETS

# SUN

RULES THE ASTROLOGICAL SIGN OF LEO

Although the Sun is officially a star, for the purpose of astrology it's considered a planet. It is also the centre of our universe and gives us both light and energy; our lives are dependent on it and it embodies our creative life force. As a life giver, the Sun is considered a masculine entity, the patriarch and ruler of the skies. Our sun sign is where we start our astrological journey whichever sign it falls in, and as long as we know which day of which month we were born, we have this primary knowledge.

# MOON

RULES THE ASTROLOGICAL SIGN OF CANCER

We now know that the Moon is actually a natural satellite of the Earth (the third planet from the Sun) rather than a planet but is considered such for the purposes of astrology. It's dependent on the Sun for its reflected light, and it is only through their celestial relationship that we can see it. In this way, the Moon in each of our birth charts depicts the feminine energy to balance the masculine Sun's life force, the ying to its yang. It is not an impotent or subservient presence, particularly when you consider how it gives the world's oceans their tides, the relentless energy of the ebb and flow powering up the seas. The Moon's energy also helps illuminate our unconscious desires, helping to bring these to the service of our self-knowledge.

# MERCURY

Mercury, messenger of the gods, has always been associated with speed and agility, whether in body or mind. Because of this, Mercury is considered to be the planet of quick wit and anything requiring verbal dexterity and the application of intelligence. Those with Mercury prominent in their chart love exchanging and debating ideas and telling stories (often with a tendency to embellish the truth of a situation), making them prominent in professions where these qualities are valuable.

Astronomically, Mercury is the closest planet to the Sun and moves around a lot in our skies. What's also relevant is that several times a year Mercury appears to be retrograde (see page 99) which has the effect of slowing down or disrupting its influence.

# VENUS

The goddess of beauty, love and pleasure. Venus is
the second planet from the Sun and benefits from
this proximity, having received its positive vibes.
Depending on which astrological sign Venus falls in
your chart will influence how you relate to art and
culture and the opposite sex. The characteristics of
this sign will tell you all you need to know about
what you aspire to, where you seek and how you
experience pleasure, along with the types of lover you
attract. Again, partly depending on where it's placed,
Venus can sometimes increase self-indulgence which
can be a less positive aspect of a hedonistic life.

# MARS

RULES THE ASTROLOGICAL SIGN OF ARIES

This big, powerful planet is fourth from the Sun and exerts an energetic force, powering up the characteristics of the astrological sign in which it falls in your chart. This will tell you how you assert yourself, whether your anger flares or smoulders, what might stir your passion and how you express your sexual desires. Mars will show you what works best for you to turn ideas into action, the sort of energy you might need to see something through and how your independent spirit can be most effectively engaged.

# JUPITER

Big, bountiful Jupiter is the largest planet in our solar
system and fifth from the Sun. It heralds optimism,
generosity and general benevolence. Whichever sign
Jupiter falls in in your chart is where you will find
the characteristics for your particular experience of
luck, happiness and good fortune. Jupiter will show
you which areas to focus on to gain the most and
best from your life. Wherever Jupiter appears in your
chart it will bring a positive influence and when it's
prominent in our skies we all benefit.

# SATURN

RULES THE ASTROLOGICAL SIGN OF CAPRICORN

Saturn is considered akin to Old Father Time, with all the patience, realism and wisdom that archetype evokes. Sometimes called the taskmaster of the skies, its influence is all about how we handle responsibility and it requires that we graft and apply ourselves in order to learn life's lessons. The sixth planet from the Sun, Saturn's 'return' (see page 100) to its place in an individual's birth chart occurs approximately every 28 years. How self-disciplined you are about overcoming opposition or adversity will be influenced by the characteristics of the sign in which this powerful planet falls in your chart.

# URANUS

RULES THE ASTROLOGICAL SIGN OF AQUARIUS

The seventh planet from the Sun, Uranus is the planet of unpredictability, change and surprise, and whether you love or loathe the impact of Uranus will depend in part on which astrological sign it influences in your chart. How you respond to its influence is entirely up to the characteristics of the sign it occupies in your chart. Whether you see the change it heralds as a gift or a curse is up to you, but because it takes seven years to travel through a sign, its presence in a sign can influence a generation.

# NEPTUNE

Neptune ruled the sea, and this planet is all about deep waters of mystery, imagination and secrets. It's also representative of our spiritual side so the characteristics of whichever astrological sign it occupies in your chart will influence how this plays out in your life. Neptune is the eighth planet from the Sun and its influence can be subtle and mysterious. The astrological sign in which it falls in your chart will indicate how you realise your vision, dream and goals. The only precaution is if it falls in an equally watery sign, creating a potential difficulty in distinguishing between fantasy and reality.

# PLUTO

RULES THE ASTROLOGICAL SIGN OF SCORPIO

Pluto is the furthest planet from the Sun and exerts a regenerative energy that transforms but often requires destruction to erase what's come before in order to begin again. Its energy often lies dormant and then erupts, so the astrological sign in which it falls will have a bearing on how this might play out in your chart. Transformation can be very positive but also very painful. When Pluto's influence is strong, change occurs and how you react or respond to this will be very individual. Don't fear it, but reflect on how to use its energy to your benefit.

# YOUR SUN SIGN

Your sun or zodiac sign is the one in which you were born, determined by the date of your birth. Your sun sign is ruled by a specific planet. For example, Scorpio is ruled by Pluto but Gemini by Mercury, so we already have the first piece of information and the first piece of our individual jigsaw puzzle.

The next piece of the jigsaw is understanding that the energy of a particular planet in your birth chart (see page 78) plays out via the characteristics of the astrological sign in which it's positioned, and this is hugely valuable in understanding some of the patterns of your life. You may have your Sun in Scorpio, and a good insight into the characteristics of this sign, but what if you have Neptune in Leo? Or Venus in Aries? Uranus in Virgo? Understanding the impact of these influences can help you reflect on the way you react or respond and the choices you can make, helping to ensure more positive outcomes.

If, for example, with Uranus in Taurus you are resistant to change, remind yourself that change is inevitable and can be positive, allowing you to work with it rather than against its influence. If you have Neptune in Virgo, it will bring a more spiritual element to this practical earth sign, while Mercury in Aquarius will enhance the predictive element of your analysis and judgement. The scope and range and useful aspect of having this knowledge is just the beginning of how you can utilise astrology to live your best life.

# PLANETS IN TRANSIT

In addition, the planets do not stay still. They are said to transit (move) through the course of an astrological year. Those closest to us, like Mercury, transit quite regularly (every 88 days), while those further away, like Pluto, take much longer, in this case 248 years to come full circle. So the effects of each planet can vary depending on their position and this is why we hear astrologers talk about someone's Saturn return (see page 100), Mercury retrograde (see page 99) or about Capricorn (or other sun sign) 'weather'. This is indicative of an influence that can be anticipated and worked with and is both universal and personal. The shifting positions of the planets bring an influence to bear on each of us, linked to the position of our own planetary influences and how these have a bearing on each other. If you understand the nature of these planetary influences you can begin to work with, rather than against, them and this information can be very much to your benefit. First, though, you need to take a look at the component parts of astrology, the pieces of your personal jigsaw, then you'll have the information you need to make sense of how your sun sign might be affected during the changing patterns of the planets.

# YOUR BIRTH CHART

With the date, time and place of birth, you can easily find out where your (or anyone else's) planets are positioned from an online astrological chart programme (see page 110). This will give you an exact sun sign position, which you probably already know, but it can also be useful if you think you were born 'on the cusp' because it will give you an *exact* indication of what sign you were born in. In addition, this natal chart will tell you your Ascendant sign, which sign your Moon is in, along with the other planets specific to your personal and completely individual chart and the Houses (see page 81) in which the astrological signs are positioned.

A birth chart is divided into 12 sections, representing each of the 12 Houses (see pages 82–85) with your Ascendant or Rising sign always positioned in the 1st House, and the other 11 Houses running counter-clockwise from one to 12.

# ASCENDANT OR RISING SIGN

Your Ascendant is a first, important part of the complexity of an individual birth chart. While your sun sign gives you an indication of the personality you will inhabit through the course of your life, it is your Ascendant or Rising sign – which is the sign rising at the break of dawn on the Eastern horizon at the time and on the date of your birth – that often gives a truer indication of how you will project your personality and consequently how the world sees you. So even though you were born a sun sign Scorpio, whatever sign your Ascendant is in, for example Cancer, will be read through the characteristics of this astrological sign.

Your Ascendant is always in your 1st House, which is the House of the Self (see page 82) and the other houses always follow the same consecutive astrological order. So if, for example, your Ascendant is Leo, then your second house is in Virgo, your third house in Libra, and so on. Each house has its own characteristics but how these will play out in your individual chart will be influenced by the sign positioned in it.

Opposite your Ascendant is your Descendant sign, positioned in the 7th House (see page 84) and this shows what you look for in a partnership, your complementary 'other half' as it were. There's always something intriguing about what the Descendant can help us to understand, and it's worth knowing yours and being on the lookout for it when considering a long-term marital or business partnership.

# THE
# 12
# HOUSES

While each of the 12 Houses represent different aspects of our lives, they are also ruled by one of the 12 astrological signs, giving each house its specific characteristics. When we discover, for example, that we have Capricorn in the 12th House, this might suggest a pragmatic or practical approach to spirituality. Or, if you had Gemini in your 6th House, this might suggest a rather airy approach to organisation.

# 1ST HOUSE

### RULED BY ARIES

The first impression you give walking into a room, how you like to be seen, your sense of self and the energy with which you approach life.

# 2ND HOUSE

### RULED BY TAURUS

What you value, including what you own that provides your material security; your self-value and work ethic, how you earn your income.

# 3RD HOUSE

### RULED BY GEMINI

How you communicate through words, deeds and gestures; also how you learn and function in a group, including within your own family.

# 4 TH HOUSE

### RULED BY CANCER

This is about your home, your security
and how you take care of yourself and
your family; and also about those family
traditions you hold dear.

# 5 TH HOUSE

### RULED BY LEO

Creativity in all its forms, including fun
and eroticism, intimate relationships and
procreation, self-expression
and positive fulfilment.

# 6 TH HOUSE

### RULED BY VIRGO

How you organise your daily routine, your
health, your business affairs, and how you
are of service to others, from those
in your family to the workplace.

# 7 TH HOUSE

### RULED BY LIBRA

This is about partnerships and shared
goals, whether marital or in business,
and what we look for in these to
complement ourselves.

# 8 TH HOUSE

### RULED BY SCORPIO

Regeneration, through death and rebirth,
and also our legacy and how this might be
realised through sex, procreation
and progeny.

# 9 TH HOUSE

### RULED BY SAGITTARIUS

Our world view, cultures outside our
own and the bigger picture beyond our
immediate horizon, to which we travel
either in body or mind.

# 10TH HOUSE

### RULED BY CAPRICORN

Our aims and ambitions in life, what we aspire to and what we're prepared to do to achieve it; this is how we approach our working lives.

# 11TH HOUSE

### RULED BY AQUARIUS

The house of humanity and our friendships, our relationships with the wider world, our tribe or group to which we feel an affiliation.

# 12TH HOUSE

### RULED BY PISCES

Our spiritual side resides here. Whether this is religious or not, it embodies our inner life, beliefs and the deeper connections we forge.

# THE FOUR
# ELEMENTS

The 12 astrological signs are divided into four groups, representing the four elements: fire, water, earth and air. This gives each of the three signs in each group additional characteristics.

# FIRE

ARIES ❧ LEO ❧ SAGITTARIUS

Embodying warmth, spontaneity and enthusiasm.

♏

# WATER

## CANCER ❧ SCORPIO ❧ PISCES

Embodying a more feeling, spiritual and intuitive side.

# EARTH

TAURUS ❧ VIRGO ❧ CAPRICORN

Grounded and sure-footed and sometimes rather stubborn.

# AIR

GEMINI ❧ LIBRA ❧ AQUARIUS

Flourishing in the world of vision, ideas and perception.

# FIXED, CARDINAL OR MUTABLE?

The 12 signs are further divided into three groups of four, giving additional characteristics of being fixed, cardinal or mutable. These represent the way in which they respond to situations.

# FIXED

### TAURUS, LEO, SCORPIO AND AQUARIUS ARE FIXED SIGNS

Their energy tends to be steady and they are less reactive, more responsive, although they can have a tendency to be resistant to change and need encouragement.

# CARDINAL

### ARIES, CANCER, LIBRA AND CAPRICORN ARE CARDINAL SIGNS

Their energy is often instinctive and action-oriented, enabling them to get things started, although there's sometimes a tendency to fail to carry things through.

# MUTABLE

### GEMINI, VIRGO, SAGITTARIUS AND PISCES ARE MUTABLE SIGNS

The clue here is their adaptability and responsiveness to change, which they don't fear, and readiness to listen to and embrace new ideas.

# MERCURY RETROGRADE

This occurs several times over the astrological year and lasts for around four weeks, with a shadow week either side (a quick Google search will tell you the forthcoming dates). It's important what sign Mercury is in while it's retrograde, because its impact will be affected by the characteristics of that sign. For example, if Mercury is retrograde in Gemini, the sign of communication that is ruled by Mercury, the effect will be keenly felt in all areas of communication. However, if Mercury is retrograde in Aquarius, which rules the house of friendships and relationships, this may keenly affect our communication with large groups, or if in Sagittarius, which rules the house of travel, it could affect travel itineraries and encourage us to check our documents carefully.

Mercury retrograde can also be seen as an opportunity to pause, review or reconsider ideas and plans, to regroup, recalibrate and recuperate, and generally to take stock of where we are and how we might proceed. In our fast-paced 24/7 lives, Mercury retrograde can often be a useful opportunity to slow down and allow ourselves space to restore some necessary equilibrium.

# SATURN RETURN

When the planet Saturn returns to the place in your chart that it occupied at the time of your birth, it has an impact. This occurs roughly every 28 years, so we can see immediately that it correlates with ages that we consider representative of different life stages and when we might anticipate change or adjustment to a different era. At 28 we can be considered at full adult maturity, probably established in our careers and relationships, maybe with children; at 56 we have reached middle age and are possibly at another of life's crossroads; and at 84, we might be considered at the full height of our wisdom, our lives almost complete. If you know the time and place of your birth date, an online Saturn return calculator can give you the exact timing.

It will also be useful to identify in which astrological sign Saturn falls in your chart, which will help you reflect on its influence, as both influences can be very illuminating about how you will experience and manage the impact of its return. Often the time leading up to a personal Saturn return is a demanding one, but the lessons learnt help inform the decisions made about how to progress your own goals. Don't fear this period, but work with its influence: knowledge is power and Saturn has a powerful energy you can harness should you choose.

# THE MINOR PLANETS

Sun sign astrology seldom makes mention of these 'minor' planets that also orbit the Sun, but increasingly their subtle influence is being referenced. If you have had your birth chart done (if you know your birth time and place you can do this online) you will have access to this additional information.

Like the 10 main planets on the previous pages, these 18 minor entities will also be positioned in an astrological sign, bringing their energy to bear on these characteristics. You may, for example, have Fortuna in Leo, or Diana in Sagittarius. Look to these for their subtle influences on your birth chart and life via the sign they inhabit, all of which will serve to animate and resonate further the information you can reference on your own personal journey.

## AESCULAPIA

Jupiter's grandson and a powerful
healer, Aesculapia was taught by
Chiron and influences us in what
could be life-saving action, realised
through the characteristics of the sign
in which it falls in our chart.

## BACCHUS

Jupiter's son, Bacchus is similarly
benevolent but can sometimes lack
restraint in the pursuit of pleasure.
How this plays out in your chart is
dependent on the sign in which
it falls.

## APOLLO

Jupiter's son, gifted in art, music and
healing, Apollo rides the Sun across
the skies. His energy literally lights up
the way in which you inspire others,
characterised by the sign in which it
falls in your chart.

## CERES

Goddess of agriculture and mother of
Proserpina, Ceres is associated with
the seasons and how we manage cycles
of change in our lives. This energy is
influenced by the sign in which it falls
in our chart.

## CHIRON

Teacher of the gods, Chiron knew all about healing herbs and medical practices and he lends his energy to how we tackle the impossible or the unthinkable, that which seems difficult to do.

## DIANA

Jupiter's independent daughter was allowed to run free without the shackles of marriage. Where this falls in your birth chart will indicate what you are not prepared to sacrifice in order to conform.

## CUPID

Son of Venus. The sign into which Cupid falls will influence how you inspire love and desire in others, not always appropriately and sometimes illogically but it can still be an enduring passion.

## FORTUNA

Jupiter's daughter, who is always shown blindfolded, influences your fated role in other people's lives, how you show up for them without really understanding why, and at the right time.

## HYGEIA

Daughter of Aesculapia and also associated with health, Hygeia is about how you anticipate risk and the avoidance of unwanted outcomes. The way you do this is characterised by the sign in which Hygeia falls.

## MINERVA

Another of Jupiter's daughters, depicted by an owl, will show you via the energy given to a particular astrological sign in your chart how you show up at your most intelligent and smart. How you operate intellectually.

## JUNO

Juno was the wife of Jupiter and her position in your chart will indicate where you will make a commitment in order to feel safe and secure. It's where you might seek protection in order to flourish.

## OPS

The wife of Saturn, Ops saved the life of her son Jupiter by giving her husband a stone to eat instead of him. Her energy in our chart enables us to find positive solutions to life's demands and dilemmas.

## PANACEA

Gifted with healing powers, Panacea
provides us with a remedy for all ills
and difficulties, and how this plays
out in your life will depend on the
characteristics of the astrological sign
in which her energy falls.

## PSYCHE

Psyche, Venus' daughter-in-law, shows
us that part of ourselves that is easy to
love and endures through adversity,
and your soul that survives death and
flies free, like the butterfly that
depicts her.

## PROSERPINA

Daughter of Ceres, abducted by Pluto,
Proserpina has to spend her life divided
between earth and the underworld and
she represents how we bridge the gulf
between different and difficult aspects
of our lives.

## SALACIA

Neptune's wife, Salacia stands on
the seashore bridging land and sea,
happily bridging the two realities.
In your chart, she shows how you
can harmoniously bring two sides of
yourself together.

## VESTA

Daughter of Saturn, Vesta's job was
to protect Rome and in turn she
was protected by vestal virgins. Her
energy influences how we manage our
relationships with competitive females
and male authority figures.

## VULCAN

Vulcan was a blacksmith who knew
how to control fire and fashion metal
into shape, and through the sign in
which it falls in your chart will show
you how you control your passion and
make it work for you.

# FURTHER READING

*Jung's Studies in Astrology: Prophecies, Magic and the Qualities of Time*,

Liz Greene, Routledge (2018)

*Lunar Oracle: Harness the Power of the Moon*,

Liberty Phi, OH Editions (2021)

*Metaphysics of Astrology: Why Astrology Works*,

Ivan Antic, Independently published (2020)

*Parkers' Astrology: The Definitive Guide to Using Astrology in Every Aspect
of Your Life*,

Julia and Derek Parker, Dorling Kindersley (2020)

## USEFUL WEBSITES

Alicebellastrology.com
Astro.com
Astrology.com
Cafeastrology.com
Costarastrology.com
Jessicaadams.com

## USEFUL APPS

Astro Future
Co-Star
Moon
Sanctuary
Time Nomad
Time Passages

## ACKNOWLEDGEMENTS

Thanks are due to my Taurean publisher Kate Pollard for commissioning this Astrology Oracle series, to Piscean Matt Tomlinson for his careful editing, and to Evi O Studio for their beautiful design and illustrations.

## ABOUT THE AUTHOR

As a sun sign Aquarius Liberty Phi loves to explore the world and has lived on three different continents, currently residing in North America. Their Gemini moon inspires them to communicate their love of astrology and other esoteric practices while Leo rising helps energise them. Their first publication, also released by OH Editions, is a box set of 36 oracle cards and accompanying guide, entitled *Lunar Oracle: Harness the Power of the Moon*.

Published in 2023 by OH Editions,
an imprint of Welbeck Non-Fiction Ltd,
part of the Welbeck Publishing Group.
Offices in London, 20 Mortimer Street, London, W1T 3JW,
and Sydney, 205 Commonwealth Street, Surry Hills, 2010.
www.welbeckpublishing.com

Design © 2023 OH Editions
Text © 2023 Liberty Phi
Illustrations © 2023 Evi O. Studio

A CIP catalogue record for this book is available from the British Library.

ISBN 978-1-80453-000-9

Publisher: Kate Pollard
Editor: Sophie Elletson
In-house editor: Matt Tomlinson
Designer: Evi O. Studio
Illustrator: Evi O. Studio
Production controller: Jess Brisley
Printed and bound by Leo Paper

MIX
Paper | Supporting
responsible forestry
FSC® C020056
www.fsc.org

10 9 8 7 6 5 4 3 2 1